Team Talk

Sheila M. Blackburn

The second book in Set A of
Sam's Football Stories

Dedication
For My Mum.
With thanks to Tom for all the support
and understanding.

Ackowledgements
With thanks to *The Boots Company* and *Delmar Press in Nantwich*,
for their support of this project.

Published by Brilliant Publications
1 Church View
Sparrow Hall Farm
Edlesborough
Dunstable
Beds LU6 2ES

Telephone: 01525 229720
Fax: 01525 229725
e-mail: sales@brilliantpublications.co.uk
website: www.brilliantpublications.co.uk

Written by Sheila M. Blackburn
Illustrated by Tony O'Donnell of Graham Cameron Illustration

© Sheila M. Blackburn 2002

ISBN 1 903853 192 Set A – 6 titles: Football Crazy, Team Talk, Will Monday Ever Come?, Training Night, If Only Dad Could See Us! and A Place on the Team.
ISBN 1 903853 036 Set B – 6 titles: The First Match, Trouble for Foz, What about the Girls?, What's Worrying Eddie?, Nowhere to Train and Are We the Champions?

Printed in England by Ashford Colour Press Ltd
First published in 2002
10 9 8 7 6 5 4 3 2 1

Sam was so excited.

Eddie Ford was going to run a football team.
He said it was for Sam and his friends.
Eddie was going to find a place to do training.
He was going to fix up some matches.

It was just what Sam had always wanted.
He had to tell his friends at once.
Sam ran round to Danny's house.

Sam's Football Stories

Danny was having tea in front of the TV.

"Danny! Danny! Guess what?"

"Oh, Sam, it's you. Come in," said Danny's mum.
"Danny's watching TV. Go through to him."

"Danny! Guess what?" said Sam. "You know
Mrs Ford? Well, her son, Eddie, wants to run
a football team for us!"

Danny stopped eating his chips and looked at Sam.
"For us?" he said.

"Yes, us! For you and me and Rob and Mouse
and all the others."

"Are you sure?"

"Look, Danny – he's round at our house now.
He's talking to my mum. Come and see him if
you like."

Danny looked at Sam's face.

"For real?" he asked.

"Sure, it's for real," said Sam.

"Mum says we can have a meeting at our house. Bring your mum and dad. Monday at 7 o'clock."

"This is it, then," said Danny.

"Yeah!"

"Ace!" said Danny. "Have a chip."

That night after tea, Sam sat at the table
in the kitchen.

"What are you doing?" asked Dad.

"Making a list," said Sam.

"Is it a team list?"

"Right," said Sam. "I've put down all the
ones I saw before tea."

"How many?" asked Dad.

Sam counted:
Danny,
David,
Jon,
Rob,
Mouse,
and me – that makes six so far," he said.

"No rush," said Mum. "You've got all weekend."

"I still need to see Tim, Foz, Shamir,
and Ben," said Sam.

"Not now – it's getting dark," said Dad.
"Plenty of time tomorrow."

"Not really," said Sam.

"Why not?" asked Mum. "Tomorrow is Saturday.
What else have you got to do?"

"Training," said Sam.
"I have to do some football training."

"I might have guessed," said Dad.
"However, you still can't go out tonight."

Sam went up to his room to read some
football books.

Team Talk

On Saturday morning, Sam woke up early.

He lay in bed thinking.
Two days at home, then a whole day at school,
then the meeting!

He couldn't wait.

Sam got out of bed and went to the window.

Oh no! It was raining!
It was pouring down.
Sam felt very cross.

He wanted to do some football training.

At breakfast, Sam said,
"Can I go to Danny's?"

"Sam, it's raining hard," said Mum.
"Come shopping with us in the car."

"No, thank you!" said Sam.
He got his coat on.

"I can stay at Danny's house until it stops."

"If it stops at all today," said Dad.

"It will stop. It must," said Sam.
"We just have to do some training."

He ran out.

Mum and Dad looked at each other and smiled.

Sam and Danny went up to Danny's room.
They looked at some old football programmes.
They swapped some football stickers.
Sam's sticker book was nearly full.

"Boys! The rain has stopped!" called Danny's mum.
Sam and Danny ran downstairs and outside.

They had to go and see Tim, Foz,
Shamir and Ben to tell them the news.

After dinner, some of the boys got together.
They went down to the wasteland.
It was near Mrs Ford's shop.

"We need to do some training," said Sam.

"OK. What shall we do?" asked Tim.
"Pass the ball to each other and tackle –

all that sort of stuff,"
said Sam.

"Why not just have
a game?" said Foz.

So they did.

The wasteland was muddy.

Foz fell over and got covered in mud.

Tim fell over Foz and cut his leg.

He went home crying.

Then it started to rain again.

The game was over.

Sam and Danny walked home.

"It's good, this football training, isn't it?" said Sam.

"You bet," said Danny.
"Can't wait till the meeting."

"See you on Monday," said Sam.

Sam's Football Stories

On Sunday, Sam had to go
with Mum and Dad to see Gran.
They set off after dinner.

Gran was pleased to see them.
She gave Sam a big hug.

"I've got something to tell you," said Sam.
He told Gran about the team.

"That's nice, dear," said Gran.
She didn't know much about football,
but she did make very good cakes.
Sam was glad that they were staying for tea.

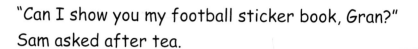

"Can I show you my football sticker book, Gran?"
Sam asked after tea.

"That would be nice," said Gran.
"I'll look at the pictures."

Soon it was time to go home.

"I hope the meeting goes well," said Gran.

"Thanks, Gran. It will," said Sam.

Sam's Football Stories

Monday was a very, very, very long day.

"Will it ever end?" Sam said to Danny in class.

"Get on with your work," said Miss Hill.

"How long is it till 7 o'clock?" asked Danny.

"Ages," said Sam.

"Boys! Get on with your work, or you will have to miss break!"

They did their work.

They wanted to play football at break!

Sam ran all the way home after school.

Mum was busy in the kitchen.
"You can't eat those cakes," she said.

"Why not?" said Sam. "They look good."

"They are for the meeting, not for you!"

"Mum, it's a meeting about a football team,
not about cakes!"

Sam's Football Stories

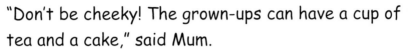

"Don't be cheeky! The grown-ups can have a cup of tea and a cake," said Mum.
"So ... hands off!"

Sam got the room ready at 6 o'clock.

Dad came home from work.

The time went very slowly for Sam. He looked at a few football books, but he was too excited to sit still.

Sam's Football Stories

Eddie came on his old bike just before 7 o'clock.

"Have you got some good news?" asked Sam.

"Wait and see," said Eddie.

At 7 o'clock, the room was full.
Some of the grown-ups had to stay in the kitchen.

Eddie said hello.

He told them about being at college.
Then he said the lads could have a team.

"We can go to the Scout Hut on Mondays.
We can do our training on their field,
or go inside if it's wet."

The boys cheered.

"When can we start?" asked Sam.

"Next week," said Eddie.

"Six till seven. Bring your kit."

"How much will it cost?" Danny asked.

"Not much. Just a bit each week for the hut.
I'll tell you next Monday."

Team Talk

"Will we get to play some matches?"
Sam just had to ask.

"Yes, I think so," said Eddie.
"I have to talk to some people to fix it all up.
Leave it to me. I'll let you know when you come
to training."

Eddie looked round the room.
"Is that all OK?" he wanted to know.

"Yes!" shouted the boys.

That night, Sam lay under his United bed cover.

"It was a good meeting," said Mum.
"You will get your team."

"You must be very pleased," said Dad.

"Yeah – great!" said Sam, yawning.

"Goodnight, then. Sleep tight."

But Sam was already fast asleep.

We hope that you enjoyed this book. To find out what happens next? Look for the next book in the series.

Set A

Football Crazy
Team Talk
Will Monday Ever Come?
Training Night
If Only Dad Could See Us!
A Place on the Team

Set B

The First Match
Trouble for Foz
What about the Girls?
What's Worrying Eddie?
Nowhere to Train
Are We the Champions?